Hello MONEY

By the end of this book, you will have created Multiple Streams of Passive Income on a Shoestring Budget that will be put on Autopilot & that you can run in less than 1 hour per day. Hello Laptop Lifestyle!

WELCOME TO THE FIRST DAY OF THE REST OF YOUR LIFE

Let's Do This!

Let's Get Started

Create Your Electronic Real Estate Portfolio

The number of people earning over $1,000 online **increased 42.2% from 2019 to 2020!**
Do you know how you climb a mountain?
One little step at a time!
You do not look up at the mountain,
you just keep climbing.
You are wasting precious time looking for the "Perfect Method" or "Magic Bullet". I eventually learned most of the people who make money online--use MULTIPLE methods!
This Guide is set up as Day 1, Day 2, etc. but don't worry if a task takes you more than a day.
If you don't quit, this book can change your life.
Just keep going & don't quit!
You can come back to each day or take extra time on each "Day". Just go at your own pace but don't look up at the mountain. Just keep climbing!
FOCUS on only 1 day at a time then mark it off & celebrate your progress!
This book contains affiliate links that provide you discounts and I may earn a commission at no additional cost to you:)

Overview

1. FAST TRACK
2. WEBSITE SETUP
3. EBOOKS
4. FUNNELS
5. YOUTUBE
6. ETSY
7. TSHIRTS
8. COURSES
9. AUDIOBOOKS
10. AUTO RESPONDER
11. SOCIAL MEDIA
12. CANVA
13. VIDEOS
14. AFFILIATE LINKS
15. YOUTUBE CREATION
16. ARTICLES
17. COFFEE MUGS
18. ANNOUNCE-MENTS
19. PLR BOOKS
20. CREATE DESIGNS
21. WEDDING ANNOUNCEMENTS
22. JEWELRY DESIGN
23. COLORING BOOKS
24. COACHING
25. UGC
26. CREATION
27+. CREATION
31+. CREATION & MARKETING

Day 1
Fast Track

The Fast Track Digital Asset is a Business in a Box & gives you an instant high ticket affiliate digital product the very next day. The Fast Track Method is optional but allowed me to "hit the ground running".

You want to start with a Digital asset that gives you 100% of the commission from day 1 which is what put me in profit quickly. The <u>Fast Track Method</u> has a one-time fee upfront but No monthly fee and a low entry point which makes it appeal to everyone. The majority of the rest of the digital assets you will be creating on Day 2-30 are free or cheap to create. Just go to mydailypaybusiness.com to get the Fast Track Digital Asset set up.

Once you finish setting up the Fast Track method above (optional), you will just take your first 10-30 minutes a day and follow the step-by-step instructions included in the Fast Track Digital Asset. There are very few Business Owners who can say they only need to spend 1 hour a day on their Business. But that is exactly what we are creating! **Want to take a day or a week off**--no problem you are your own boss!

The instructions on there show you **how to set it up on Autopilot and work less than 1 hour a day. It only takes me about <u>10 minutes a day now</u>.** It's easy!

Day 1 Fast Track

Your only "job" will be to create 3 videos of 6-10 seconds long on CapCut (free) and upload them to TikTok. You don't even have to show your face if you don't want to!

Just film anything for 6-10 seconds (see the <u>Idea List</u> below, showing your face is optional), then put words directing traffic to your new website you create using the step-by-step instructions provided with the Fast Track Digital Asset.

You can use the **Magic Tool** to Auto Post **those videos to 6 platforms**: Tiktok, Pinterest, YouTube, FaceBook Reels, Twitter, & Instagram Reels. Pinterest, YouTube, and Tiktok are all search engines so you want as many on posts on there as possible and be sure to add keywords so they are all searchable the rest of your life! To access the **Magic Tool** just go to: https://tinyurl.com/3pjnyk5u

If you don't want to use the <u>Magic Tool</u> (optional) to auto-post, you can just post them manually on each platform 3x/day. It's more time consuming, but its free. Consistency is critical!

That tool saves me so much time and is one of the ONLY monthly fees I pay to run this entire business virtually on auto-pilot :)

Day 1 Fast Track

Do not worry about **number of views** your videos get the first couple months. Even with only 200 views per video, with 6 platforms thats 1200 people seeing each video. For Free! And you are doing 3 videos a day. Thats 3600 views from videos you made ONCE but that will be online the rest of your life! This is why it's *critical* to be consistent.

With the Capcut app I can make all 3 videos for the day in 10 minutes. The more you do it the faster you will get. Sometimes I make a bunch in a day and then just save them in the TikTok drafts. That way I have a whole weeks worths of videos and I can take the whole week off! Then I just click "post" on one of my drafts at breakfast, lunch, and dinner. The **Magic Tool** above then auto-posts those 3 videos to all 6 platforms on auto-pilot!

I don't think it gets much easier than that.

Plus don't forget all the videos you have previcusly posted...are still out there working for you! You don't lift a finger, yet your business is out there working on auto-pilot for you.
This has been life-changing for me!
Posts I did 6 months ago and had completely forgotten about are just now making it up in the search results and producing traffic.

Day 1 Fast Track

I recommend not starting to post until you have 20+ videos saved in drafts. That way it is easy to stay ahead and to be **consistent**. For the first few months do NOT skip days-consistency is what counts. It's so easy and you create many at once to plan ahead for days you may be too busy. Then just post them 3x/day. Before you know it, it will start to snowball :

The first month, the only thing you will be looking for with the videos is patterns. Just look through your videos and notice which colors, fonts, length of video, people in the video, pets in the video, upbeat vibe, chill vibe, sounds, time of day, small font, big font, etc that does the best. Just **notice patterns** so you can **combine them** later for greater and greater success. Keep track of patterns in a file and save sounds that do well so you can re-use them.

Day 1 Fast Track

Before you start creating videos, go to Tiktok's search feature. Type in different terms like "make money online", "affiliate marketing", "digital marketing", etc. Then filter the results by different things like most views, most likes, most recent, all time, etc. Look for ideas, common themes, sounds that did well, the font they used, the color schemes, the length of the video, etc. Don't copy their videos. Just get ideas and notice themes and patterns.

Not sure what to make your videos about and **don't want to show your face?**

Use "**Ghost Commerce**" and post videos of anything you want in the background that could be interesting to people, then add your words on top of it.
Here's some ideas for scenes in the background:
--vacations
--colorful food
--typing on a keyboard
--coffee cups with inspirational sayings
--cooking
--doing art
--pets
--walking / working out
--even cleaning!

Pair the video with a Viral Sound by searching "viral sounds" on TikTok.

Day 1
Fast Track

I now only "work" less than 1 hour per day!

If I want to take a day off or a week off, I do!

Your only "job" once you create the digital assets, will be to create the 3 videos a day. Then post them on all 6 platforms using the **Magic Tool** on page 6.
Or go to: https://tinyurl.com/3pjnyk5u

Those videos will be online forever!

By the end of this book, you will have set up Multiple Streams of Income on a Shoestring Budget that will be
put on Autopilot &
that you can run in less than
1 hour per day.
Hello Laptop Lifestyle!

Day 2
Website Setup

Today you will **Create Your Main Website.** You will add a picture of the Fast Track Digital Asset as well as each digital asset you create on day 2-30. Then you will only have 1 website to send traffic to.

Go **HERE** to create your **Website** using one of the pre-built templates. You can use any service you want to create a website but I found that one to be really simple and it has great done-for-you templates to pick from. Also their support is the best I've found so far. You will then just **add pictures of each new digital asset you create to the website you create**. Then you will have one central place where ALL of your asset are.

Just add the basic info to the Website for now.
You will use this as a **Central Spot** for all your other Pieces of Electronic Real Estate you are about to create. (See the next page for setup Instructions.)

Create the site one time and get paid Forever!
Don't over-think it. Keep it simple for now.
You will add more to it as we go. Just get the structure of the site in place, pick a template, select the colors you want, etc.

Day 2

Website Setup

You are putting a puzzle together one little puzzle piece at a time. If you walk in a construction site you may get really overwhelmed. Keep your thoughts focused on the Big Picture. Anytime you get overwhelmed or frustrated, visualize the whole puzzle put together!
Time Freedom.
Financial Freedom.
Location Freedom

I used a done-for-you template using the **link** above and then just chose my colors and added my products over time.

Let's Set Up Your Main Website:

1. Pick a Domain name on <u>Godaddy.com</u> Select a <u>GENERAL</u> website name like Liveyourbestlife.com that will allow you to put a variety of things on your website like living healthy, making money, etc. This only costs me about $12/year. I don't add any of the upgrades but you can if you want.

Day 2

Website Setup

2. Go **HERE** to **Set up your website**. You don't need to do much today--you will ADD each piece of electronic real estate to your website later as you go through each day of the course. This will create a CENTRAL SPOT so then you only have to market one site not many products to your audience.
You can also use this link:
https://tiryurl.com/43dr9fxx

Creating a website is easy! You will just select a pre-made template then change the text, add each digital asset (you'll do that later), and insert the link that takes them to the product.

Selecting a Template:
For my website I chose "Wordpress + Woocommerce", and the Theme selected is "NewStore" but you can use one you like best. I added Elementor later which just puts everything in blocks and made it easier to design a nice attractive site.

3. Design Your Site using Free Images from **pexels.com Unsplash.com or pixabay.com** or your own pictures.
You d*on't need to do much today, you are just getting your website set up.*
Then you can add your pieces of Electronic Real Estate to your site later as you create each one.

4. Set up your Blog on your website or blogger.com to be used LATER to write articles and add your affiliate links for free traffic. Just familiarize yourself with how blogging works today.
We will cover it more later, but here's a simple overview:

~research what topics and search terms are high volume and low competition
~write a blog post
~add search terms & SEO
~add your links to your website, digital assets, or affiliate products

Day 2 — Website

Later you will **add Posts to your Blog about interesting topics that will lead traffic back to your Main Website. You will write the articles once but it can lead traffic to your site <u>Forever</u>!**

I have blog posts I wrote literally years ago that still bring hundreds of visitors to my site. Just be sure to enter the keywords and spend time on SEO so they will eventually come up in search results. Keep in mind, those are posts that took me no more than 1 hour to write ONE TIME. I've never done a single other thing to them. Yet they still bring me traffic!

You will just have one Central Spot to direct traffic to but it will house multiple streams of income.

Don't get overwhelmed and don't give up. You only have to create them ONCE then you are set up for life!

Day 3

E-books

Ebooks are easy!
You can use one of these 2 Softwares:

https://bookbolt.io/2200.html

https://tinyurl.com/w7hkzcm2

to Create Ebooks and Activity Books FAST!

They have tons of pre-built templates for blank journals, planners, children's books, how-to books, etc. You can also use Canva to create Ebooks if you don't want to use the done-for-you Templates.

You don't have to be an expert to write an ebook. You just have to know more than your reader about any topic. Everyone knows something other people don't!

Create the ebook ONCE. Open up a whole new stream of Reward!

The Software makes it super simple
but it is optional, it just helped me create multiple Ebooks fast with pre-built templates!

You don't need to **write ebooks today.**
You are just getting everything **set up**, researching ideas, and learning how to do it.

Day 3

E-books

You can earn money from the <u>sale of books and ebooks</u> on Amazon. You can **ALSO** <u>earn per page that is read</u> of each of your ebooks on Kindle. Imagine when you have 100 small ebooks!

You can even use **Fiverr.com** to pay someone to write the ebook for you if you want.
Everyone knows a lot about something!
Pick a topic you are interested in and just give your best tips Most people appeciate "real talk" instead of a bunch of super "professional" blather that is over their head!

Save yourself a lot of time and **do your RESEARCH** before your start your ebook.

1. Go on Amazon and see what topics are the bestsellers in the ebook categories.
2. Go to **Wordstream.com** and **Erank.com** type in some keywords to see what kind of topics people are already searching for. You are trying to find search terms with high volume but low competition.

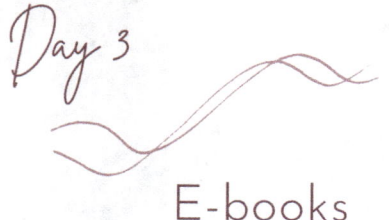

E-books

E-book Step by Step **Set-up**:

1. Go to https://kdp.amazon.com to create a free **KDP account** to add your future ebooks to. Here's a step-by-step setup video: https://youtu.be/BSUMkRac24E

2. On KDP you will create the book listing, let them assign you an ISBN number than add that to the last page of your book and ebook.

3. Upload your **ebook** file that you created using one of the Softwares above or on Canva as a print-preview.

4. Then use the Creator Tool on KDP to create the Ebook <u>**Cover**</u> or design your own on <u>Canva</u>.

On KDP you will upload the book and the cover SEPARATELY as 2 different files.

E-books

E-book **Set-up**:
I had a terrible time calculating the correct sizes using the amazon kdp 'instructions' so I'm going to save you a lot of time and include the ones that worked for me here:
Here's your Cheat sheet!
Paperbacks:
6 x 9 book
12.698 x 9.250 cover

8.5 x 11 book
17.848 x 11.250 cover

8.5 x 8.5 book
17.325 x 8.75 cover

Remember on printed books, the cover has to wrap all the way around the front and back of the book.
On Ebooks, it will just cover the front.
So for **Ebooks Covers**,
2560 (height) x 1600 (width) px
(1:6:1 ratio)

Day 3
E-books

5. Or you can **use CANVA to create your ebook** using this step-by-step **Canva VIDEO tutorial** click **HERE** or go to: https://youtu.be/AsYFtEqlUfE

I use the pro version of Canva which is $6/month but you can use the free version. I think the pro is worth it because then you can access a lot more graphics & features.

6. Later you will **Upload your ebook** PDF (the book) & then **Upload your ebook COVER** to your new free KDP amazon account.

(Today you are just setting up everything up and familiarizing yourself with everything.)

7. Research: use the keyword research tools shown in this book to research what kind of books sell and find popular keywords. If you selelct long keywords that people are ALREADY SEARCHING FOR and design your book title around that you get much better results.

E-books

Don't get overwhelmed and don't give up. You only have to do this ONCE then you are set up for life!

<u>PRO TIP</u>:
Whether you use one of the Softwares that create Ebooks quickly or use Canva and do it yourself, you will have 2 steps--create the actual book and create the cover.
You will upload the cover and the actual book separately to KDP to get your ebook on Amazon where millions of people shop every day!

To see a step-by-step **Video** on **how to upload them to KDP** you can go here:
https://youtu.be/BSUMkRac24E

Before writing ebooks, **do your research** on wordstream.com or erank.com to find topics with high search volume and low competition. You can also search on Amazon and see what kind of books are top sellers.
If no one is searching for your book, you will write it for nothing.

E-books

Solve a problem or provide an answer and you have an instant audience who is already searching for you. If you create an ebook you also can get paid by Amazon per page that people read.
You may not need this page.
I am including it because I had trouble creating my first ebook, so here is an alternate method if you are not using the done-for-you software shown above.

1. Add your ebook file (download as a PDF Print if using Canva) to Adobe Acrobat Pro.
2. Click FILE, then "Reduce Size"
3. Save it and click the box that says "reduce file size"
4. Then upload that reduced file to KINDLE CREATE.
5. On Kindle Create, click:
   --New, Choose, Print Replica, Choose file, select your reduced file PDF to upload, click GENERATE or Export, click OK, rename as your "reduced Ebook KPF", save
6. Upload to KDP as an e-book
7. Upload the cover as a JPG
   Ebook cover 2560 x 1600 px
   image should be 50MB or smaller.

The only thing you will do today is **set up your Funnel to start gathering your leads** on autopilot so you can go enjoy your life!

If you did not already do so on Day 1, **create a FREE funnel** or go here: https://tinyurl.com/2x6kdurz

This will put an all-inclusive system in place to capture all of your leads.

Click **HERE** to set up your **Free Funnel**. If you did the Fast track method, a full series of pre-written follow-up emails were added to your Funnel in the Fast Track Instructions. If you did not, you can write your own email series to automatically go out to people who show interest in your digital assets

***Your funnel and subscriber list will eventually became one of your most VALUABLE assets!

To watch a **step-by-step video** on setting up the Funnel click **Here**

Or go to https://youtu.be/clDuge-p7Aw

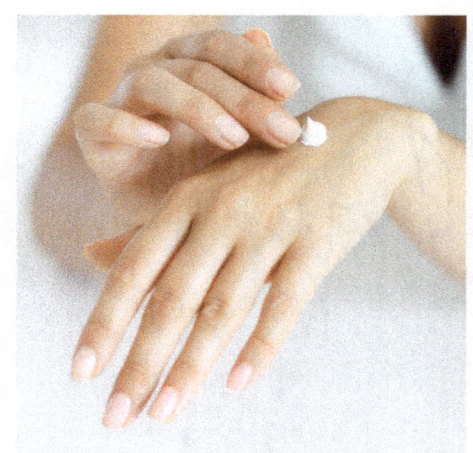

Day 4

Funnels

You will then add general text, but don't add much yet as it will change as you move through the 30 days.
Don't get overwhelmed and don't give up. You only have to do this ONCE then you are set up for life!

Funnels take the guesswork out for potential buyers. It guides them through the sales process to free you up to enjoy your life!

Another simple way to sell your Digital Assets is to create a **Stan Store** instead of a website, that also has a powerful **Funnel** included that you can use to sell courses, gather emails, & link to your TikTok!
Or go to: https://tinyurl.com/3yuvv8p7

Day 5 — YouTube Setup

Create a YouTube Channel. You won't be creating videos yet, just getting the channel set up.
You won't need to show your face if you don't want to.
You will be creating videos ONE-TIME (then they will be online Forever) and these can be a serious source of Long-Term passive income for years to come.

In the future, you can do **Explainer Videos** of top software or products people are already searching for an add your affiliate links or **links to your Digital Assets**.

You can also do **Product Comparisons** and **add your affiliate links** in the description.

Day 5

YouTube Setup

Each video you create will have Affiliate Links that will direct people to your website. Over time those will be snowballing but you will not be doing any additional work!

Create the video once & reap a lifetime of free traffic!

You will upload your TikTok videos or do it AUTOmatically with the **MAGIC TOOL** to literally run Your YouTube channel with zero work on your part!

Plus later, as your channel gets more popular, you can get paid per view from YouTube and also get paid for ads placed in the videos.

Boost Your YouTube Video Rankings:

Once you decide what videos you want to create, you can **Boost Your Video Rankings** using this Ranking software or go here:

https://tinyurl.com/yfpuskdh

You will not be designing the whole store today. You will just **set up your Etsy store** to be ready for your future designs!
To watch a step-by-step **video** on setting up an Etsy store just click **HERE** or go to: https://youtu.be/3JzlCRC4W1c
Right now you are just **selecting a GENERAL name for your Etsy store** (like ChangeYourLife) that will allow you to add content later.

You will add the text/description later. Right now you are setting up your store to use later. The setup is free!

Tomorrow you will link your new Etsy store to your new Printify store to automatically list the tshirts/Tanks/Sweatshirt designs you will be creating.
Don't get overwhelmed and don't give up. You only have to do this ONCE then you are set up for life!

Day 7 Tshirts

You will not be designing the actual tshirts today. Go to **Printify.com and set up an account then link it to your Etsy store** you created at Etsy.com Then everything will be ready and set up for your future tshirt designs! It will virtually run on autopilot once you set it all up.

You will add more text/description/products to your store later. Right now you are just setting up your Printify account and linking it to your Etsy account to be ready for the designs you create.

To create your first T-shirt design for free you can go to Canva.com and select CUSTOM size 3873 x 4814 px and then download the design as a PNG. Be sure to **click the box** that says **"Transparent"** so only your actual design downloads.

I use the Pro version of Canva for $6 a month because I use Canva for many, many things & feel its definately worth it! But you can just use the free version if you want. Then just look on Etsy for ideas & start designing! You'll more designs in the future, just get the hang of it today.

Before you start designing shirts, do some research!

Go to Amazon, Ebay, and Etsy to see what the top selling designs are in various categories.

It may not be what you think!

Often it's things that don't even take much creativity like 2 words--Stay strong.
Or Best Dad. Or Bug Off. Or Dog Mama.
Do your research before you start! You can use the **Keyword Research Chart** to keep track of all of your Research.

To make your Etsy Store successful, you can go on Erank.com and find keywords that are HIGH in Search Volume, but LOW in Etsy competition.
To watch a **Step-by-step Video** on Using Erank to find Etsy keywords and Optimize your listings just click **HERE** or go to
https://youtu.be/zKr0BgTh1s8

Day 7
Tshirts

To see a step by step video on how to create a tshirt design on Canva click **HERE** or go to: https://youtu.be/tKD0xoDefu4

TIP: Select "Transparent Background" on Canva to remove the rectangle color background and just have your design put on the tshirt

To watch a Video on **how to navigate Printify and select products** to add your design to on Printify click HERE or https://youtu.be/n9HXLnVjaQU

To upload your first product onto Printify click **HERE** to watch a step by step **Video** or go to: https://youtu.be/wrqieuFJBeg

You don't need to start designing tshirts yet, but you can go on Etsy & Amazon to start getting an idea of what is selling.

Don't get overwhelmed and don't give up. You only have to **create them ONCE** then you are set up for life!

Day 7

Keyword Research

NUMBER OF MONTHLY SEARCHES	KEYWORDS	COMPETITION: HIGH, MED, LOW	USE	DON'T USE
			○	○
			○	○
			○	○
			○	○
			○	○
			○	○
			○	○
			○	○
			○	○
			○	○
			○	○
			○	○
			○	○
			○	○
			○	○
			○	○
			○	○
			○	○
			○	○
			○	○
			○	○
			○	○
			○	○
			○	○

You will save yourself months of time if you do not skip this step.

Brainstorm:
Write down all niches that interest you. For now this is just a brainstorm list.

Day 7

Keyword Research

Keyword Research

NUMBER OF MONTHLY SEARCHES	KEYWORDS	COMPETITION: HIGH, MED, LOW	USE	DON'T USE
			○	○
			○	○
			○	○
			○	○
			○	○
			○	○
			○	○
			○	○
			○	○
			○	○
			○	○
			○	○
			○	○
			○	○
			○	○
			○	○
			○	○
			○	○
			○	○
			○	○
			○	○

<u>Research:</u>
You are then going to **head to wordstream.com** and do the actual research. You can **use my Free Worksheet to do your Keyword Research**

The goal is to find keywords that people are searching for but that don't already have a lot of competition. If you see things like "Where to buy ___" that tells you people are searching for that and trying to spend money. You want keywords with high searches per month and low competition. Just start plugging words in!

Day 8
Courses

Create an Online Course. This is going to take more than 1 day. <u>Use today just to come up with an idea</u>.

Everyone knows something other people don't. Watch YouTube videos on course creation and research ideas today using the keyword Research chart on the previous page.

Go to: <u>answerthepublic.com</u> & <u>Quora.com</u> and make a list of what people are asking about. Then you already have an eager audience!

See what people need help with. If you are good at woodworking you can create a simple course around that. Good at make-up? Create tutorial videos. Know how to cook budget-friendly homecooked meals? Create a course for college students.

Or you can even hire someone on Fiverr.com or Upwork.com to create a course for you!

Day 8
Courses

Once you decide on a topic, you will need to **select a LMS** (Learning Management System). This is just the "machine" that will make your course available on your website to your audience.

Click <u>HERE</u> to go to a drag and drop course builder to create your first simple course. Or you can go to: https://tinyurl.com/j5pa8yju

Don't make it too complicated! People like simple straightforward classes and they respond to practical everyday things that help them change their life for the better.

I created a course 5 years ago that took me 2 weeks.
It is now one of my greatest sources of passive income!

Take your time and do a good job. It's a one time committment

Day 8 Courses

Marketing Your Course

Options:

1. You can put your course **on your website**. This gives you full control of the content and 100% of the profit. The drawback is then you do all the advertise the course to get traffic to your site.

2. You can list the course **on Udemy** or a similar site. This gives you instant traffic but they take a great deal of the profits.

3. You can also sell your course by Creating a **Stan Store** that contains a funnel to drive your traffic to buy your course. You can add your Stan Store Link to your TikTok account bio. Once you have 1000 subscribers, your link will become clickable. This will make it simple for the free traffic your 3 videos a day brings in, to buy your course & signup for your emails. If you go with a Stan Store, it will have a funnel to drive traffic.

Create the course one-time.

Reap the benefit for a Lifetime!

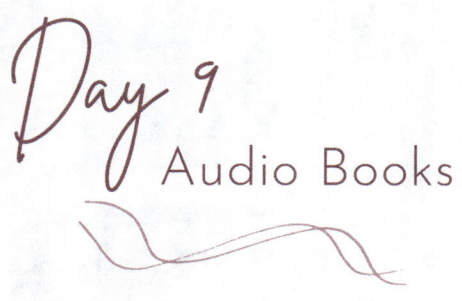

To create an Audio Book, Set up an account on <u>ACX.com</u> Almost half of all Americans listened to an audiobook last year and the audiobook market is nearly 3.5 billon dollars!

The audiobook market is growing at a rate of 30% per year, which nearly quadruples the growth rate for eBooks.

You will **Read the text out loud <u>One Time</u> & Earn Money from it Forever!**

There are several ways you can benefit from audiobooks.

1.**Record yourself reading** your book and list it as audiobook for sale.

Day 9
Audio Books

2. You can also **create a listing on Fiverr** or Upwork to record audio for other peoples books and get paid great money!

3. If you want to hire someone on Fivver or Upwork to record your ebook into an audiobook: a high-quality audiobook can generally be recorded at the rate of about $300 per 10,000 words. But then you will earn the money from the purchases of them audiobook forever!

Auto Responder

Let me start by saying setting up your Autoresponder Campaigns and Email series can be a pain and a lot of work.

However, it can play a MAJOR role in making your online business VERY hands-off.
So roll your sleeves up today and just knock it out!

If you purchased the Fast Track Digitial Asset, it comes with a full Email Series, thus most of the work is already done for you. The instructions in there show you step-by-step how to set it up on auto-pilot.

If you did not purchase the Fast Track, you will just be writing your own follow-up email series to automatically go out to people once they show interest in your digital assets.

Auto Responder

You have 2 options.
1. Use the same AutoResponder you set up with the FastTrack method but create a 2nd Campaign & Email Series for your other digital assets. That way if someone inquires about the Fast Track Digitial Asset, they will get one series of emails (that came with the Fast Track Digital Asset) to encourage them to make a purchase. And then the second campaign can be set up so if someone shows interest in your other digital assets, they will get a separate set of emails.
2. Option 2: Click <u>HERE</u> to set up a second different autoresponder if you want to keep them separate. Then you can keep everything separate. You will have one autoresponder for those interested in the Fast Track digital. And a second one for those who show interest in your website.
Or go to: https://tinyurl.com/pxxvfa4y

Auto Responder

It will take some time, but you only have to do it ONCE! This will help your Business be on Autopilot!

You will be sleeping, and people will be able to respond to emails you set up that went out on Autopilot, make a purchase, and you just wake up to the Payment Notification!

When someone shows interest in one of your digital assets, affiliate products, tshirts, ebooks you can **include a form on your website for them to fill out** to receive your newletter, blog posts, coupons, etc
The you can set up 10-20 emails to go out on a schedule on Autopilot to each person who signs up to your Autoresponder by filling out the form on your website!
The **Rule of 7** says it takes people seeing something 7 times before they buy it. That is where your Auto-responder comes in.
This can create a lifetime of passive income!
With NO additional work on your part!

Day 11

Automate Social Media

Today you will take one of the most important steps to truly PASSIVE income so you can go enjoy your life! You will be **automating your social media posts**. Take one day, link them all up to your website, blog, and auto-responder.

1. Click **HERE** to AUTO POSTS on Social Media! This software will literally **CREATE posts for you** and **autopost them** on Instagram, Pinterest, Twitter, etc. Just get it set up today, you will add content later. Once you add future **products** to your website, the software **will automatic upload them** & new posts will be **automatically created** featuring each new product! (This optional)
Or go here: https://tinyurl.com/3v9p7b8j

2. Then click **HERE** to easily **AUTO POST pins** you create on Canva onto Pinterest. Just get it set up you will add content later. You can schedule a month of pins & schedule them to pin on other boards as well. (Optional)
Or go here: https://tinyurl.com/2xsanume

These 2 steps play a huge part in our goal to **AUTOMATE your business** to make it truly Passive Income!

Day 11

Automate Social Media

PINTEREST is free & your posts will now be scheduled out for months at a time using the tool above!

Then you can just go enjoy your life!

Organize & schedule all of your social media posts using the links on previous page.

Then you will be able to maintain your on-going marketing of your digital assests from anywhere in the world!

Just get your account set up today. ****You will create a month of posts later for each digital product you create. You can create awesome Pinterest posts on Canva..

Day 12

Create Designs on Canva

Today you will **Create a Free Canva account** if you have not done so & begin learning how to design amazing posts for your Pinterest Pins & Instagram Posts that link to your website, blog, and affiliate links.

In Canva you can **create T-shirt designs to upload to Printify**. Then you will just send the tshirt designs to your Etsy store, Ebay, and/or to your website you created so that people can purchase them & receive them on **autopilot**!

You can even Click on Youtube Thumbnails in Canva to **create attention-getting thumbnails** for your YouTube Videos!
Pinterest Pins, Instagram posts, and Youtube videos give you Free Advertising. (More on this later)
There are a lot of great Canva tutorials with tips and tricks on YouTube. **Watch tutorials today**.

Day 13
Videos

Practice using Video Editing software today. Use today to watch videos to learn and get good at it!

Click HERE to check out **the creation studio** to learn how to easily create marketing videos, YouTube videos, add transitions, add sound clips, trim clips, etc.
Or go here: https://tinyurl.com/2s4zfdnk

Just **play around with video creation** today. Practice on Canva & Invideo today and watch tutorials until you get good at it. Just pick a topic and start creating and editing.

Watch some YouTube Tutorials Videos today.

People love videos & motion!
Create the videos ONE-TIME and they can earn you money for a Lifetime!
--70% of Instagram users watch stories daily.
-- 25% of Gen Z and Millennials use stories to find products and services.
--Influencers are paid between $43 and $721 for IG stories they are so powerful!

Day 14
Affiliate Links

Set up your **Clickbank** and **WarriorPlus** account. Narrow down which affiliate categories and products you like and could link to. Write an article or blog post 1 time, then it will be in Cyber Space forever to be available to earn you recurring monthly commissions!

Be sure to change the search results to rank the affiliate products based on "gravity" (at least 50 or higher) and look for products with **residual monthly income. Health, wealth, and relationships are the most popular.**

Overall 2020 affiliate earnings in the United States increased by **67%** over 2019.

In 2020, there was a **66.4% increase in brand-new earners** (affiliates who never earned an affiliate paycheck before

Day 14
Affiliate Links

Research these Affiliate products and pick 3 to start with:

Yogaburn

Resurge

Venus Factor

Flat Belly Tonic

ProDentim

AlpiLean

JavaBurn

Then you will just create Pins, Posts, Videos, Reels, Shorts, Tiktoks and write articles/posts then insert your Affiliate links. For some platforms they do not allow affiliate links. So instead just direct traffic to your website with the affiliate link and picture of the product on there.

Day 14

Affiliate Links pt 2

Today you will **Set up your Amazon, Walmart, and Ebay Affiliate Accounts**.

Just set the accounts up.
You can add content later.

You can then:
--do product reviews
--do product ranks (Top 10 airfryers, etc)
~~ list your products on there
~~ link your printify products to Ebay
~~ place ads on your website with high ticket commission payouts that link to Amazon or Walmart
~~place links on your YouTube videos with high ticket commission payouts
~~send Free Traffic to your ebooks, audio books, digital products, and tshirt designs that you created One Time. Millions of people are on these website to spend money.

Millions of people are on these website to spend money.

Day 15

YouTube Video Creation

Create your first YouTube videos today. You can do one that in under 5 minutes. People are busy & like short videos.

Here are 2 softwares I use to make videos a lot faster!

You can click **HERE** to create amazing professional videos in 3 clicks! Or go to: https://tinyurl.com/5n7psvc5

Or click **HERE** to create videos in minutes with no technology knowledge needed! Or go to: https://tinyurl.com/2s4zfdnk

They are both optional softwares and just expedite the process of creating a lot of videos to get them out there quickly. Remember you make the videos once and they will be out there working for your FOREVER!

Day 15

YouTube Video Creation

Take today to research keywords, explore YouTube for trends, watch tutorials, select the software you will create the videos on, etc.

1. A great first video is an **explainer video**.
Pick a software or Product you like or are familar with and that has an affiliate commision and just explain how to use the product in simple terms.
Show only your screen if you are camera shy.
Or do a comparison video of 2 products and link to them in the description.

2. Another great place to start is a **ranking video**. You can do "Top 3 _____" (airfryers, vacuums, software, laptops, etc) and just include one of the products you have an affiliate link for. Then you will include the affiliate link in the description.
If you are an Amazon Affiliate you can include multiple product affiliate links.

Day 15

YouTube Video Creation

Create quality videos that you would want to watch. You can earn money from adding affiliate links, including a product comparisions or features in your video, and paid advertisers that pay per view once your channel takes off. You can even use Fiverr to hire others to create videos for you!

Avoid getting your channel shut down:
--Do NOT make any promises or guarantees (You have no idea whether people will implement the info so you can't guarantee they are going to succeed.)

Take your time and add the max number of keywords so your video is searchable for years.
Watch a couple videos for how to correctly post videos to maximize your success.

Set on Autopilot
The 3 short videos a day can be uploaded to YouTube as Reels automatically using the Magic Tool or manually each day.
The Magic Tool uploads the video automatically for me which basically **created my whole YouTube channel with no additional work on my part**! To access it go to:
https://tinyurl.com/3pjnyk5u

Day 16 Articles

<u>Simple overview for Articles:</u>

~research what topics and search terms are high volume and low competition
~write a blog post or articles
~add search terms & SEO
~add your links to your website, digital assets, or affiliate products

For passive income write articles such as "Top 10 Best Airfryers" etc with affiliate links to Amazon or Walmart that will be in Cyberspace forever! You will write the article, add your affiliate links, and post the articles on your website or other places. Articles I wrote years ago still get traffic!

Write it once. Get Paid Forever.

You can also click <u>HERE</u> to get Paid to Write Articles. Look over these sites that will pay you to write articles to earn some quick cash to cover any expenses you have while you build your Real Estate Empire!
Or click here: <u>https://tinyurl.com/2p98en2d</u>

Day 17
Coffee Mugs

Design coffee mugs & upload to Printify. Go on Amazon or Ebay for ideas of what is selling. Narrow down which products you like. These can be created in minutes but be in cyberspace forever!

Go on Canva & get creative!
Design coffee mugs 1 time, they will be in Cyber Space forever to earn you recurring monthly commissions!

Use the Keyword Research Tool I gave you to **do your Research of Top Sellers before you get started**!

Once you create your design you can **upload it to printify** and link it to your Etsy store, redbubble, and Ebay store. You can also list it on your website by syncing Printify with your website, Etsy, and Ebay. You can also upload your designs for Free onto Redbubble which puts each design on a bunch of different products like hats, purses, shirts, art, bath mats, socks, etc!

Day 18

Baby Announcements

Design Baby Announcements & Baby Shower invites, etc on canva.
Upload your Digital Assets to Etsy.

Go on Etsy for ideas of what is selling.
Narrow down which products you like. Go on Canva & get creative!

You can **connect them to _Corjl_** to **process the orders for you on AUTOPILOT** and **allow the buyer to add their personal details** like the babys due date etc.

Design them 1 time, they will be in Cyber Space forever to earn you recurring monthly commissions!

These are Digital Downloads. So unlike Physical products like T-shirts, you get to keep all of the money!

Here is a 3 min step-by-step YouTube video

Day 19
PLR Books

Use PLR software to access ebooks that you don't write but can earn commission on!

Go here to get Setup:
https://tinyurl.com/747s4e98

Private Label and Resell ebooks can be it's own source of passive income for you!

You can list them on your website, post links to them in your YouTube video descriptions, etc.
Here is an explainer <u>Video</u> on using PLR books to earn passive income.
https://youtu.be/ge3Td1-puWc

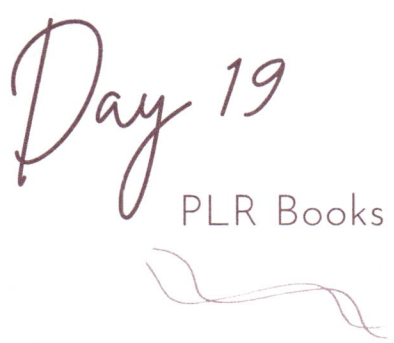

Day 19
PLR Books

You can also use PLR ebooks to download the PDF, then edit it to **include your affiliate products or links** that you got from Clickbanks.

You don't write the ebook but can earn commission on it!

Then create pins to advertise the ebook.

For example, you take a free PLR book like "Fit, Fab & 50", and then you add your affiliate links to "The Smoothie Diet" from Clickbanks to use PLR books to earn passive income.
Then just write articles and post them on your website or on sites like Medium.com

Day 20
Create Designs

Today you will create designs to be added to journals, daily planners, tshirts, mugs, etc. Then you can upload the designs to Printify, Redbubble, and Amazon KDP.

This will be something you can do long-term as new ideas pop in your head.

Today try to create a few to get your started. Research what is selling first using the instruction that were given earlier, Wordstream, askthepublic.com and the Keyword Researcher Chart. Do you think your shirt for "women" or "gnome lovers" has the best chance of making it to the top of the search results?

If you create multipurpose designs, like a Sunflower, you can use that on daily planners, tshirts, coffee mugs, etc. So you created 1 design but can spin many products off that design that only took a few minutes of your day!

Create designs ONCE, sell them on autopilot forever!

Day 21
Wedding Announcements

Today you will focus on creating Wedding Shower & Wedding announcements on Canva.

Then **upload them to Corjl** to process the orders for you on **Autopilot** through Etsy.

Design them 1 time, then they will be in Cyber Space forever to earn you recurring monthly commissions!

These are Digital Downloads. So unlike Physical products like T-shirts, you get to keep all of the money (minus any fees)!

Be sure to do your Research before you start designing!

Digital downloads are some of the highest profit margin and a great place to spend your time creating them one time. A design that took you 1 hour can produce sales for you a year from now when you completely forget you made it!

Day 22

Jewelry Design & Metal Art

Today you will research jewelry drop-shipping.
You can design it through ShineOn.
You don't actually design the jewelry. **You just design the decorative card the jewelry lays on using Canva.**

You can also create Metal Art by going to Precisionmetalartusa.com these do really well especially at the holidays and can be personalized.

You can then link the design to your Etsy store, Ebay store & your website. Once you design it & create the listing the orders are processed pretty much on auto-pilot!

You design it once.
Link it to Etsy, Ebay, & Your Website.
Then people can buy it forever!

Now You've Created another income stream and the potential to Collect Passive Income for Life!

Coloring Books

You can use Canva to create black and white coloring pages as a digital asset to sell on Etsy as well as Coloring Books on Amazon. They are very popular for children & Adults!

Digital downloads are great way to make passive income because there is no physical product so it is all profit.

It is free to create, free to upload to Etsy and only 0.20 to list on Etsy. You can create adult coloring pages or children's coloring pages. Both have a lot of potential! Be certain to use the Keyword Research Chart to see what sells before you start creating.
Here is a step-by-step **VIDEO** to create coloring pages for Etsy.

Step-by-step
1. Go to Canva.com and click Create a design 8.5 x 11
2. Click on Elements select images to color
3. Change the image colors from pink/purple,etc to Black and white or search "black and white images"
4. Add Text then change the font to HOLLOW (color black) or SPLICE (color white, offset 0) so the words can be colored in
5. If you want to, you can add tiny numbers and make it color by number with a color code key at the bottom

Day 24
Coaching

Coaching will be something that you can focus on in the future once you finish the other areas we have covered.
As you go along your journey you are going to learn so much!

In order to do Coaching you don't need to know everything.
You just need to be further along and know more than the person reaching out to you.
You can learn more about this later just keep it as a possible source of passive income for your portfolio!
You can add a 1-on-1 consult as a "product" on your website.
You can do speaking or co-host events or podcasts!

User Generated Content is another great way to earn money online. It's not a strictly passive form of income but it can be done from anywhere as well as genereate a lot of money for a small amount of work!

With UGC you don't need a following. You create content/do a product review,etc for a company and they post it on their platform.

Click **HERE** to watch a step-by-step video on UGC!
https://youtu.be/lqxiY85AkYA

You can learn more about this later just keep it as a possible source of passive income for your portfolio!

Day 26-30
Creation

Now you will just use the previous information and focus on creating affiliate links, designing products, writing mini-courses, creating digital wedding & baby announcements, making videos, designing digital assets and working on the other projects previously mentioned.

By the end of the 30 days you should have a strong Electronic Real Estate Portolio and many streams of passive income set up!

Now you just need to:
Be Consistent.
Be Patient!

Read those last 2 lines again.
They are difference between those who succeed and those who do not!

Day 26-30 Creation

~~**Create multiple Ebooks** fast with pre-built templates!
Click **HERE** to Create multiple Ebooks fast!
Or go to: https://bookbolt.io/2200.html

Click **HERE** for the other software I use to create ebooks and other digital assets fast!
Or go to: http://tinyurl.com/w7hkzcm2

Then just upload them to KDP Amazon. Put a picture of them on your website with a link to your Author Profile. Then you can create pins on Pinterest with keywords about your ebook or digital asset. Pinterest has 445 million monthly active users! Pins are free to create. Remember Pinterest is a search engine. So pins you forgot you created can get views indefinately to create a life time of passive income!

Day 26-30 Creation

~~Be sure you have Set up your Clickbank and WarriorPlus accounts and be looking for affiliate products to add to your portfolio on your website and social media. Affiliate marketing takes time but then it can snowball from all the seeds you put in the ground!

~~Keep Creating designs on Canva & add them to Printify & Redbubble, then just link Printify to your Etsy/Website/Ebay.

The Top Goal is Automation.

Then you can go enjoy your life and wait for all the seeds you have sown in CyberSpace to start sprouting!

You have put everything you created on one website.

1. Click **HERE** to AUTO POSTS **Product Images** on Social Media. Or go to: https://tinyurl.com/3v9p7b8j
Once you set that up, every time you add a product to your website, it will sync and **create social media posts on autopilot**! Then you have very little to do each day to keep your passive income rolling in!

2. Then set up the **Magic Tool** or go to: https://tinyurl.com/3pjnyk5u
That software will **Autopost the 3 videos** you make per day on 6 platforms thus creating 18 videos a day for you!
These 2 steps AUTOMATE your business to make it truly Passive Income! These are both optional but will be a complete game changer in making your business more & more Passive!

More Tips & Tricks

#1 TikTok is the Fastest growing free marketing platform. Create 3 short TikToks & then set them up on Auto-pilot to post to 6 different platforms. This way you create ONE video, post it several places, and your "work" for the day is done! It only takes me about 10 minutes a day on the free AutoCut App.
After you finish the Creation phase...

Your only job:
1. Create 3 short TikTok videos
2. Post the Videos
3. Use the **Magic Tool** to Auto post it to 6 Platforms!

Now you have 3 short videos a day X 6 plaforms =
18 videos per day.
126 videos per week.
6552 videos per year!

More Tips & Tricks

#2 Find Your Audience

On TikTok go to the search feature & type in words that could be your audience. TikTok will suggest others that may be a better fit.

You need to TELL the algorigthm who your audience is. You do this by:

--Using correct hashtags
--saying the keywords in your video
--using the words on the text on the screen
--using it in your description
--using it in the comments

#3
Use Hooks

~Catch them off guard
-Offer a suggestion
-Use something funny, scary or surprising
~Make them laugh, cry, or make them mad
~End with a Call to Action "Share this with someone who needs a laugh today"

More Tips & Tricks

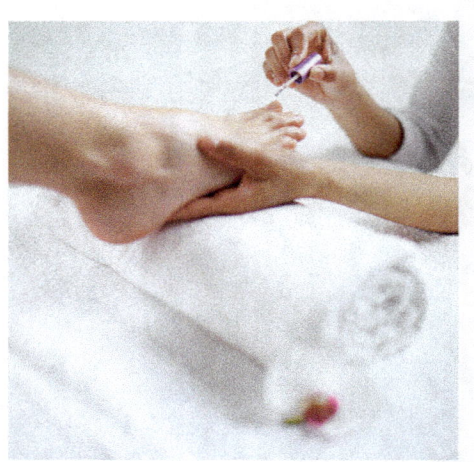

#4 Batch Your Content
You do NOT have to make content everyday! You can take 1 hour, make a bunch of videos, then repurpose them with different text to make a bunch of different video with different text, different background music, different endings, etc.

#5
Use your Schedulers & Auto-posters
Modern technology is fascinating--use it! You can create & post a month or more of content and schedule it out so you can go enjoy your life!

More Tips & Tricks

#6 Create Mockups

Your can purchase "mockups" on Etsy or create your own.
These help people see your product (an ebook, tshirt, coffee mug, coloring book, etc) being used in real life.
Save each of these mockups.
Turn them into Pinterest pins, Instagram posts, etc.
Saving them in a folder makes it super fast to post a month of pins/posts by just adding 1-2 each day on the month calendar to post on autopilot!

THEN the next month, you can even use them again by changing the color or background.
This way you have less and less to do as time goes on.

More Tips & Tricks

#7 Professional Videos
If you are recording your videos on an Iphone, go into your Settings, scroll down to Camera change the Record Video setting from 1080p to 4K at 30fps

#8 Search Trending Sounds
Use trending sounds, then go to the videos created using that sound and see how they performed. Trick: Pick one that did well in many videos, then add text to the video so TikTok can index your video into the searches.

#9 Repurpose Your Videos
Re-use videos by covering whatever was going on in the background with new text that takes up the whole screen and is set to a new trending sound. If you are using the Magic Tool it automatically removes the TikTok watermark so you can easily repurpose videos!

#10 ERank.com

I have used ERank.com a great deal to:

~ get the inside scoop on Trends,
~Understand whats working for the competition,
~Discover what people are searching for
~knowing what Month each item is likely to perform the best
~find keywords with high search volume & low competition
~Understand Holiday trends and how to get out in front of them

#11 **Stan Store**

Creating a Stan Store really simplified things for me. Your fans will have a super simple way to sign up for your email list, get your free ebook, link to your website, and purchase your course all on one tiny page! Click **HERE** to create your own Stan Store.

More Tips & Tricks

#12 More TikTok Tricks

~~Optimize Your Bio! Use Keywords and Phrases so that when somebody searches on TikTok for any of those keywords your account will come up.
~~Use Covers for your Videos so when people visit your page they will want to keep watching your content & different videos which boosts you in the Algorithm
~~Use Hooks/Text in the first 3 seconds to draw people in

More Tips & Tricks

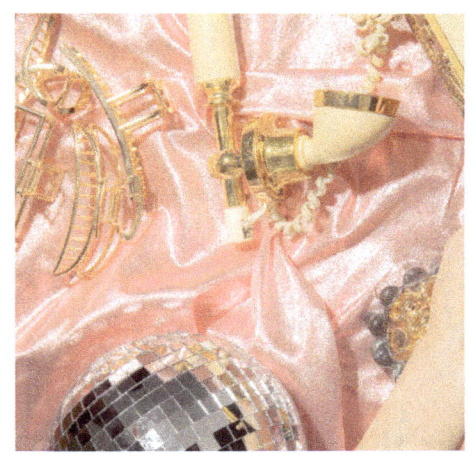

#13 More TikTok Tips: Best Times to Post*

~~Top posting time: Thursay Night at 7PM
~~Best times on each day:
Monday: 10PM
Tuesday: 9AM
Wednesday: 7AM
Thursday: 7PM
Friday: 3PM
Saturday 11AM
Sunday: 4PM

*according to Hootsuite

To personalize yours, go to your TikTok account, go to Settings, Creator Tools, Analytics, Followers and scroll down to see the peak times your followers are active!

More Tips & Tricks

#14 Tiktok Tips
~~Search your niche on TT
~~Look at the top 10 results
~~Filter by Most Liked & Past 30 Days
~~Find the common topic(s) that went viral in that niche
~~Make 10 videos on that topic
~~Make all 10 before you post the first video and save them in drafts then you are ahead and can consistent in posting
~Wait a week to see how they do
~~Don't get frustrated, it takes the algorithm 2-3 weeks to notice you
~Repeat!

More Tips & Tricks

#12 More TikTok Tricks
~~Optimize Your Bio! Use Keywords and Phrases so that when somebody searches on TikTok for any of those keywords your account will come up.
~~Use Covers for your Videos so when people visit your page they will want to keep watching your content & different videos which boosts you in the Algorithm
~~Use Hooks/Text in the first 3 seconds to draw people in

3 Steps to My Lazy Business Setup

That's it!

1. RESEARCH NICHES

2. CREATE YOUR DIGITAL ASSETS

3. CREATE 3 VIDEOS A DAY

GO ENJOY YOUR LIFE!

This book is Dedicated to my 4 amazing children who have brought an immeasureable amount of Joy to my life! You are each Inspiring in your own way and I am honored to have the priviledge of being your Mom. Follow your Dreams & Fearlessly and Passionately Pursue all that you were Created and Designed to be! Treasure Every Day, Let the Past Go, Love Openly, and Always Remember to Look for the Good in this Beautiful Life You Have Been Given!

Go Live the Life You Were Born to Live!

Create Passive Income with Digital Assets & an Electronic Real Estate Portfolio

© 2023 Deborah S. Farber. All Rights Reserved.
ISBN: 9798376552797

Copyright notice: all rights reserved. No parts of this book may be reproduced or transmitted in any form or by any means, electronic or mechanical, including photocopying and recording, or by any information storage and retrieval system, without permission in writing from the author. Warning: the unauthorized reproduction or distribution of this copyrighted work is illegal. Criminal copyright infringement, including infringement without monetary gain Is investigated by the FBI and is punishable by up to five years in prison and a fine of $250,000.

All information in this workbook is for educational purposes only and is not counseling or therapy. No guarantee or promises have been make to the usefulness of such activities nor toward any of the material in this book.

Go Live the Life You Were Born to Live

www.ingramcontent.com/pod-product-compliance
Lightning Source LLC
Chambersburg PA
CBHW050253220526
45465CB00002B/665